The British Con
the Corruption of
Parliament

The *Candour* writings of Ben Greene

by

Ben Greene

The A.K. Chesterton Trust

2017

This booklet is *The A.K. Chesterton Trust Reprint Series* No. 11

Second edition.

Printed & Published in 2017.

ISBN: 978-0-9932885-8-6

© **The A.K. Chesterton Trust, BM Candour, London, WC1N 3XX, United Kingdom.**

Website: www.candour.org.uk

Ben Greene

Contents

Foreword

A maverick by nature and a colossus in stature, Ben Greene was a gentle giant who stood six feet eight inches tall and was part of the illustrious Greene clan that included the novelist Graham Greene, Hugh Greene, Director-General of the BBC 1960-1969, and Raymond Greene, Everest mountaineer and doctor.

With an abiding interest in constitutional matters and a smouldering resentment following his questionable internment by the British government under the draconian 18b internment regulations during World War 2, he worked diligently on the subject for the rest of his life, but unfortunately died before the book he was planning was finished.

This booklet comprising five essays by Greene, which first appeared in *Candour* between 1956 and 1977, with two of them re-published under the title '*The Party System and the Corruption of Parliament*' in magazine format in 1989, is now made available once again. This second edition became necessary when I discovered an article by Ben's daughter, Leslie von Goetz[1], about the 1989 booklet. This article is now included in this work.

Never was the statement 'to stand on the shoulders of giants' more apt than when applied to the subject of this book. Long may the values he

---

[1] Leslie Greene, a long term friend of both *Candour* and the League of Empire Loyalists. She died in 2005. This article was originally published in *Candour*, Vol. XLII, Nos 7 & 8, July/August, 1990.

strived for and the insights he bequeathed to us resonate with future generations.

Rob Black

The A.K. Chesterton Trust
February 2017

THE LIFE OF BEN GREENE

by Leslie von Goetz (*nee* Greene)

BEN Greene was born in Brazil in 1901 to a reasonably wealthy family and only came to England when he was nine. The fact that English was not his first language and that he grew to the exceptional height of 6'8" combined to make him feel something of an outsider, even in his own family which included a lot of distinguished cousins such as Graham and Hugh Carleton Greene. As a result he thought deeply about the horrors of war and the injustices of society. He saw a great deal of the post-war world, doing famine relief work with the Society of Friends in Germany and the Soviet Union. He learned a lot about the reality of life in the latter country and never fell for the idealised picture. Equally he knew that the hypocrisy and wickedness had not been all on one side, either in the war or in the peace "settlement" after it, and he campaigned tirelessly for a better settlement which would be less likely to ensure the recurrence of war.

He joined the Labour Party in the interests of social justice but quickly learned that the very structure of the party, with the trade union block vote and the infiltration of Communists (in those days they were proscribed by the Labour Party), was unlikely to produce the sort of society he wanted, although he fought several constituencies in the Labour interest. When told that he was among those who would be elected to the Labour National Executive the day before the election was to take place, he refused to be a party to this kind of fraud which further strained his relations with the Labour leaders.

After The Kristallnacht

The treatment of the Jews in Germany was a matter of great international concern and Ben was sent out by the Quakers to investigate the situation as he spoke German like a native. The Dutch Prime Minister was threatening to close the frontier to Jewish refugees because of the strain they were putting on Dutch hospitality - the people who were getting out of Germany were the ones who had money and international connections, sponsorship, etc., and of course some of them turned out to be far better off than those who were scraping the barrel to offer them hospitality. In Germany Ben found the truly desperate, the ones who had lost everything and had no overseas connections.

With the help of the Red Cross, the Quakers, the Catholic and Protestant Churches and the governments concerned, a scheme was devised whereby internal relief could be given to the hardest cases inside Germany which would avoid the kind of embarrassment the Dutch had been suffering. The stumbling block, to Ben's enormous surprise, turned out to be Jews themselves. They would not agree because it meant foreign currency would be available to the Germans. This was International Finance with a vengeance! We have seen the same kind of thing in recent years in connection with South Africa, but the anti-apartheid fanatics are not usually black themselves but rather purist whites. In this case Ben could not persuade Rothschild to soften his stance. It was not that he did not believe the hardship stories Ben told him. He must have believed them for he phoned them through to Reuters in Ben's presence without checking them in any way. But then it was the same reply - no help could cross German frontiers.

The background to Ben Greene's war-time internment is rather complicated to explain in detail, and those who want to savour the truly scandalous nature of his treatment should read *The Man Who*

Was "M" - the life of Maxwell Knight by Anthony Masters, published in 1984. In summary, the fact that he was a pacifist, determined to stop the war to the best of his ability, was actually travelling to Germany and had a lot of enemies among party politicians, led MI5 to the appalling procedure of setting out to frame him.

Under Regulation 18B it was possible to detain people indefinitely without trial under one or other of two headings - "being of hostile origin or associations and by reason thereof..." or "having recently been concerned in acts prejudicial to the safety of the state and by reason thereof..." The catch for MI5 was that the Home Secretary still had to have "reasonable cause to believe" that the person concerned fell in to one or the other category. So reasonable causes were concocted by informers and agents provocateur on a scale which would have certainly embarrassed Lord Liverpool's government! Although something over 1300 were detained under these regulations, only some 750 turned out to be followers of Mosley, yet in popular memory all detainees were Mosleyites and unquestioned traitors.

A Law Unto Itself

Ben Greene was the only person detained under 18B who ever received a list of the things he was alleged to have done to have justified his detention and the grudging statement that these charges were to be "regarded as withdrawn". After two years in prison, stripped of his magistracy, a general object of odium (except curiously enough to his successful Conservative opponents in Hull and Gravesend who stood up for him valiantly), Ben Greene assumed that an action for wrongful imprisonment could only be successful. After all, an informer had concocted lies about him; he had been imprisoned on the strength of these admitted lies, so surely he had been wrongfully imprisoned? Not so, as it turned out, according to British Law as passed by our wonderful democratic House of Commons.

He did not have to prove that he had been unjustly imprisoned - rather, he had to prove that the Home Secretary had acted **unreasonably** in accepting the unsworn statements of an enemy alien. To do this, it transpired; he needed access to all the correspondence and documents which the police had removed from him years before when he was arrested. By the constant tenor of his opposition to fascism, and steadfast pacifism, he could have shown there was an element of unreason in believing he had been acting to establish a Nazi government in Britain by force of arms. But he was not given access to his own documents to prove his case - Crown privilege was pleaded - the case was lost and, to the world, because he had lost his action for wrongful imprisonment he was **not** wrongfully imprisoned.

Even his own family thought him paranoid after in his sensitivity over this slur on his reputation - his conviction that people were bringing it up behind his back, doing him down in business deals, etc. But it turned out when Anthony Masters' book came out that he had not been paranoid after all. Knight had so resented the blighting of his own career by his wrongful behaviour in Greene's case becoming known that he continued to have him watched and to try to find grounds against him.

Ben worked for years on a study of the British Constitution and how it was corrupted by the party system. He could never find a publisher - some wanted it cut down, others lengthened, while bits of it became out of date and needed to be re-written. He never got around to what might have been an even greater work: a proper study of the old legal relationship of Master and Servant and how it should have been developed to meet the new industrial conditions, without developing the trade union tyranny which was so oppressive to those without the magic card as the employer's arbitrary right of dismissal. He wanted to work in the insights of the great papal encyclicals *Rerum Novarum* and *Quadragesimo Anno*, but it did not happen.

Eventually his work on the British Constitution was published in this journal [*Candour*] and it is now available in booklet form. Ben's articles for *Candour* may be confusing for they use "sovereignty" more or less as a term of abuse, while we are accustomed to cherishing our national sovereignty. The "sovereignty" of which Ben was writing critically was the alleged ability of the British Parliament to pass any law, however contrary to the law of God, the Natural Law, or the past laws of the land, and make it the law of the land. He constantly quoted Hartley Shawcross' statement that the power of the British Parliament was such that if it were to decree that all blue-eyed babies were to be strangled at birth, then carrying out that order would not be murder[2].

The years of tragedy that have marked the retreat of empire and the establishment of "democratic self-government" over all the world have shown only too clearly how prophetically right Ben was in his condemnation of the party system allied to a "sovereign" parliament. Under this system there are **no** constraints to the tyranny of the majority. A tyrannical minority **can** be constrained by its own numerical weakness, but a democratic majority can do what it likes - and it does!

---

[2] In fact, Parliament has enacted such a decree in the guise, first, of the Abortion Act of 1967 and, very recently, of the Human Fertilisation and Embryology Bill. The latter "allows" abortion until and during birth in a wide range of cases of suspected "serious" handicap. In the view of some doctors this can include harelip or cleft palate. Laws designed to "allow" acts previously criminal are an abomination. Abortion at whatever stage is still murder and should be dealt with as such. *Rosine de Bounevialle, writing in Candour, Vol. XLII, no. 7 & 8, July August, 1990.*

THE PARTY SYSTEM AND THE CORRUPTION OF PARLIAMENT

It is now one hundred years since the modern system of disciplined and caucus controlled political Parties founded by Joseph Chamberlain and Benjamin Disraeli established a complete domination over the elected membership of the British House of Commons. This has resulted in the greatest revolution in the principles of English law and government since the dawn of English national existence. This revolution has however never been acknowledged. By retaining the forms, institutions and ceremonies of our Parliamentary heritage, though now rendered meaningless, the magnitude of the constitutional convulsion has been successfully disguised.

The English Parliamentary Constitution rested on one single principle that all authority was subject to the law of the land derived solely from the consent of the people which no ruler could change or disregard but which he was bound to administer. Based thus on the principle of the Rule of Law of the people, the English Constitution stood as the greatest achievement in the art of strong, free and stable government in the whole history of civilized mankind and as an example from which every civilized nation in the modern world has directly or indirectly sought to draw for its own national institutions.

With a legally constituted Parliament as the supreme authority, the English Constitution established the practical mechanism of a *legal* democracy by means of which the people, through the jury system, administered their own law, and by direct representation in the House of Commons controlled their own government. As Sir Lewis Namier, the historian, pointed out[3]: —

"In England since the disappearance of villeinage[4] none of the three elements of democracy was ever altogether absent. At the root of English democracy lies the right of every man to life liberty and property. To secure it was the first purpose of self government; of trial by jury and taxation by consent. The individual rights of the free born Englishman have retained their place in the political code of the nation, but in time they have come to be considered sufficiently secure, not to require constant jealous watching".

Today this great system of stable and free government survives only as an ever dwindling tradition without any legal force. With Parliament now under the absolute control of the caucus Party organization, the modern doctrine of Parliamentary sovereignty is postulated by which English law ceases to be derived from the consent of the people and is derived solely from the will and command of the Party controlled Parliament. By this doctrine of Parliamentary sovereignty, all constitutional law by which the legal supremacy of Parliament was established is nullified and with it the constitutional rights and liberties of the free born Englishman on which the Parliamentary constitution was founded. English law and government and with it English[5] destiny and welfare is now determined by the ever capricious outcome of political party rivalry.

The sole justification of the Party system is its claim that it marks the supreme development of the historic Parliamentary constitution in the establishment of Parliamentary Government as the constitutional basis of a *political* democracy. It is by virtue of this claim that all the new democracies, which have emerged in the last hundred years, except

---

[3] *Conflict — Studies in Contemporary History.* Page 187
[4] The most common type of serf, the status of peasants under the feudal system.
[5] And, of course, British.

those in the South American Republics, have followed British example in establishing their own form of Parliamentary Government. But Parliamentary Government is not the fulfilment of English Constitutional development, but its total negation.

Two hundred years ago in "*Present Discontents*", Edmund Burke[6] warned that:

"*Whenever Parliament is persuaded to assume the offices of executive government, it will lose all the confidence, love and veneration which it has ever enjoyed whilst it was supposed to be the corrective and control on the acting powers of the state. This would be the event though its conduct in such a perversion of its functions would be tolerable, just and moderate; but if it should be iniquitous, violent, full of passion, and full of faction, it would be considered as the most intolerable of all the modes of tyranny.*"

These predictions of Burke have been confirmed by the establishment of Parliamentary Government in the last hundred years. No one played a more decisive part in giving Parliamentary Government a constitutional form than A.V. Dicey[7], who as Professor of English Law at the University of Oxford published "*Lectures Introductory to the Study of the Law of the Constitution*", now generally referred to as Dicey's "*Law of the Constitution*". This work since its first publication in 1885 has been accepted as the standard authority for the doctrine of Parliamentary Sovereignty, which provided the legal basis of Parliamentary Government. In 1914 before the outbreak of the First

---

[6] **Edmund Burke** (1729 – 1797) was an Irish statesman born in Dublin; author, orator, political theorist, and philosopher, who, after moving to England, served for many years in the House of Commons of Great Britain as a member of the Whig party.
[7] **Albert Venn Dicey** (1835 – 1922) was a British jurist and constitutional theorist. He is most widely known as the author of *Introduction to the Study of the Law of the Constitution*. The principles it expounds are considered part of the uncodified British constitution.

World War, Dicey recorded in his introduction to the Eighth Edition of this work that:—

"During forty years faith in Parliamentary Government has suffered an extraordinary decline, or as some would say, a temporary eclipse. This change is visible in every civilized country."

This loss of faith was no temporary phenomenon. Professor Wade in his introduction to the Tenth Edition of the same work which appeared in 1960 remarked that:—

"It is undeniable that Parliament has suffered in the eyes of the general public a loss of prestige in the last seventy years . . . It must not be forgotten that there can be no check upon the unscrupulous use of power by a Government which finds itself in command of a majority in the House of Commons."

The latest confirmation of Burke's predictions is given with the authority of the Lord Chancellor in the Conservative Party Government. Lord Hailsham is an outspoken believer in Parliamentary Government, which he insists is the perfection of Parliamentary democracy. Yet Lord Hailsham declared that[8]:—

"It is the Parliamentary majority that has the potential for tyranny. The thing that Courts cannot protect you against is Parliament — the traditional protector of our liberties. But Parliament is constantly making mistakes and could in theory become the most oppressive instrument in the World".

The potential for tyranny confirms the total corruption of Parliamentary authority. This arises from the Party System, by which the Parliamentary majority is organised and controlled, and by which the Party Cabinet has been established as the supreme authority of the nation. The Party Cabinet has no legal or constitutional standing and

---

[8] *The Sunday Times*, 19th July, 1970.

is a secret entity of whose activities nothing is allowed to be known. It is the organ of the Party System of which we know little or nothing. What we do know is that the parties consist of private unincorporated oligarchical association under no legal or public control. Of the management and activities of these associations we know little or nothing. We know little or nothing of the rules governing these associations, though these now represent the basis of national authority. We do not know under what influences the Parties act. We have little or no information as to the sources from which the Parties derived their huge financial requirements, the sources of which must play a decisive part in Party direction. We are ignorant as to how this finance is expended.

The greatest evil of the Party System is that by its stranglehold on our Parliamentary institution, the legal democracy of our Parliamentary constitution has been suppressed. In its place the Party System has established the framework of a totalitarian authority by which the people are made subservient to their political rulers. As R.T. McKenzie[9] in his text book *"British Political Parties"* has pointed out:—

"Lip service is still paid to the classical conception of democracy even by many who are aware of the extent to which it has proved unworkable. The study of the psychology of political processes has revealed the importance of the extra-rational and irrational elements in social behaviour. The parallel development of the arts of political propaganda has enabled political leaders to exploit the irrational elements in human behaviour and to manufacture what is often a purely synthetic 'general will' so much so that some people are

---

[9] **Robert Trelford McKenzie** (1917 – 1981) was a Canadian professor of politics and sociology, and a psephologist (one who does statistical analysis of elections). He is perhaps best remembered in Britain as one of the main presenters of the BBC's General Election programmes.

prepared to argue . . . that the will of the people is the product and not the motive power of the political process."

The power of the Party system is now so absolute in all matters political that no authority, however legal, can be claimed or exercised except through the Party system itself. So absolute is the power of the Party system that anyone acting on its behalf enjoys a complete immunity from personal responsibility. However disastrous the consequences of any policy may be no-one is held personally accountable; no matter how disgraceful an event may prove, no matter how costly to the nation in life and treasure, no-one is personally culpable. We have today an immense Civil Service wielding dictatorial power in many vital departments of our national and personal life which is totally exempt from any constitutional responsibility to Parliament for the use or misuse of the power it exercises. Between it and Parliament stands a screen of professional Party politicians in the highest positions who accept a purely fictional responsibility to a Parliament under their absolute control and then only collectively.

The Party system has not only engrossed the whole authority of the nation into its own hands, but can successfully prevent the influence of any shade of opinion or the demand for the redress of grievance in Parliament; it permits only its own policy to be given effective expression. As Professor G.W. Keeton in *"Elementary Principles of Jurisprudence"* has pointed out when he wrote:—

"One of the chief differences between the modern totalitarian state and Great Britain is that the latter country provides for change in the governing party, if the electorate so decides whilst the system of the totalitarian state does not. In both cases the individual is left face to face with the sovereign authority with the balance heavily weighed against him."

But whereas the single party totalitarian system provides at least the semblance of national unity and cohesion the English Multi Party System rests upon national dissention as a principle of government.

By making national policy dependent upon the Party game, national authority rests on nothing firmer than Party expediency, unstable and fickle. The rivalry between the party organisations is activated by passion and emotion, fed by ignorance and prejudice, and is ever a focus of conflict and disruption. Under the rule of politics basic human rights are subject to the operation of forces governed by uninhibited self interest regardless of the rights of the individual and the needs of the community; only modified by political expediency, and gilded over with specious idealism in which injustice is exploited for political ends. Such a system creates in the competition for power by the various parties, and within the party organisations themselves, a constant turmoil and turbulence in national affairs, and makes impossible that stability and sense of common unity upon which alone national and even civilized progress can be achieved.

The consequence of a century of Party Cabinet Government has been catastrophic. Under our Parliamentary constitution we became the most powerful nation in the world; we became the work-shop of the world; we ruled the seas and founded a mighty empire; we were the great custodians of civil and political liberty. Since the rise of the Party Cabinet system have we retained our strength? Are we still the nation of the free? Have we succeeded in achieving unity at home or attempted a consolidation of our imperial frontiers? Has the Party Cabinet system allowed us to take advantage of the material resources of the Empire which were laid at our feet and which, with our command of the sea we could so easily have developed? No nation has ever received such a rich heritage as ours, nor been presented with such opportunities of mechanical and scientific progress in developing such an inheritance. But what have we done with all this? We played Party politics to such an extent that our Party leadership is now seeking salvation by submerging our national identity with other nations with whom we have no common heritage and whose political systems have shown a chronic instability even greater than our own. Clearly Party politics has led us into political bankruptcy and national degradation. It has led to the ruin and disintegration of our social and industrial relations. It has led us to the very verge of national extinction. As one Cabinet Minister has complacently put it:—

"Britain is now a medium sized power whose security depends upon NATO, whose economic future may lie within the expanded European Market, whose prosperity is conditioned by the world monetary system and whose industrial future is being partly shaped by huge inter-national companies with headquarters in Detroit, Eindhoven and Tokyo[10]."

To such impotence has the Party system by its corruption of Parliament reduced in a hundred years a nation which till then was the greatest imperial, industrial, commercial and financial power in the history of human civilization.

The immense fund of credit which was built up by our great historic past has in the last hundred years been systematically squandered till now it is exhausted. The realities of party politics are now upon us. The only remedy which the party system is able to propose is a coalition of the rival parties under some resounding name of national solidarity. By this means the party system can protect itself from the mutual recrimination for the collapse and failure of all its rival policies. The fact however remains that the Party system whether based on rivalry or a patched up unity is lawless and it is this lawlessness which lies at the root of our national decline. In the last hundred years under the doctrine of Parliamentary sovereignty Parliament has ceased to be the supreme control of power on behalf of the people and is now an instrument of power over the people, a

---

[10] Anthony Wedgewood Benn, *Daily Express*, 20th November, 1969.

power exercised by the Party system. Such a sovereign Parliament is incapable of supporting or maintaining the Rule of Law in England. This has been apparent to many serious observers ever since the establishment of the Party Cabinet as the governing authority of the British nation. Among these we have the testimony of no less an authority than A. V. Dicey himself. It was solely upon his work "*Law of the Constitution*" that the doctrine of Parliamentary sovereignty was received and it is solely on this doctrine that the Party Cabinet now depends. Before the wars of this century and their aftermath beclouded the constitutional issues, Dicey declared in 1914:—

"The ancient veneration for the rule of law has in England suffered during the last thirty years a marked decline. The truth of this assertion is proved by actual legislation, by the existence in some classes of a certain distrust both of the law and the judges and by some marked tendency towards the use of lawless methods for the attainment of social and political ends..."

And Dicey concludes:—

"The justification of lawlessness is in England suggested if not caused by the misdevelopment of Party Government. The Rule of Party cannot be permanently identified with the authority of the nation or with the dictates of patriotism. This fact has in recent days become so patent that eminent thinkers are to be found who certainly use language which implies that the authority or sovereignty of the nation or even the conception of the national will is a sort of political or metaphysical fiction which wise men will do well to discard."

There is for us only one alternative to the Rule of Party and that is the Rule of Law which in England rests upon the supremacy of a legally constituted Parliament. What this means is now lost to us. Today we are unable to distinguish between such opposite concepts as Parliamentary supremacy and Parliamentary sovereignty, between the consent of the people and the will of the people or between constitutional law and the constitutional lawlessness of the so called conventions of the constitution. This is no call to put the clock back. It was Coke in the reign of Elizabeth I who likened Parliament to the workings of a clock. This parliamentary clock has been made into a manipulated instrument of outside interests. What we need today is to restore the workings of this clock-like mechanism of our Parliamentary heritage. Then by lawful and legal process adjust our constitutional heritage to the requirements of our modern age.

THE PARTY SYSTEM IN BRITAIN

The British system of government based upon professional party politicians has palpably failed. By a process which Walter Bagehot[11] a century ago described as "a delicate experiment", the party politicians assumed control of the most powerful industrial, mercantile and financial nation in the world governed on principles of civil and political liberty by which all progressive thought throughout the civilized world was guided and inspired.

Today, after a century of government by party politicians, we see this vast inheritance dissipated and undermined with the British people over-taxed and over regulated and British national authority progressively reduced by impoverished impotence.

This erosion of British statesmanship in the last hundred years is the direct consequence of the modern party Cabinet system by which the party politicians have established their own absolute authority in open violation of English Constitutional principles.

These principles are founded on the free system of English laws (as the Americans described then in their Declaration of Independence) made by the consent of the English people. These principles were confirmed as a legal force in 1215 by the sealing of Magna Carta, reconfirmed in the revolution of 1399 by which Richard II was deposed, reaffirmed in 1660 by the restoration of Charles II and again confirmed in the Revolutionary Settlement after the abdication of James II in 1688, to be reaffirmed in 1784 after George III acknowledged defeat. Having successfully defeated every attempt at

---

[11] **Walter Bagehot** (1826 – 1877) was a British journalist, businessman, and essayist who wrote extensively about government, economics, and literature.

its corruption the English Constitution established itself as the foundation of strongest and most stable and responsible free national authority unequalled by that of any other community. "Let not England forget her precedence of teaching nations how to live" was Milton's famous assessment of English pre-eminence and it was the French statesman Talleyrand[12] who in the midst of the upheavals created by the French Revolution warned that "if the English Constitution is destroyed, the civilization of the world will be shaken to its foundations." The English Constitution was ever the pride and the glory of the English people.

The full significance of the English Constitution emerged at the time when all the other communities of the West including Scotland, were being subjected to the despotism of their sovereign rulers whose capricious will and commands had the full force of law. England and England alone retained her native laws by which every manifestation of arbitrary and despotic authority by Popes or Emperors or Kings or man or body of men stands condemned as lawless. To the English people arbitrary power is the root of all evil and that expresses the fundamental principle of the English Constitution.

The Kings of England were indeed sovereign but their sovereignty was under God and the law which they were sworn to administer but powerless to change. To maintain and enforce the Rule of Law of the people against rulers and subjects alike, the High Court of Parliament was instituted but so constituted that Parliament itself could not establish its own supremacy above all law. This was achieved by the fundamental condition that the overall supremacy of Parliament only became an active force on the common agreement in a written form of the three independent co-ordinate institutions of Parliament each subject to the law of the land. These were first the supreme executive

---

[12] **Charles Maurice de Talleyrand-Périgord** (1754–1838), was a French bishop, politician and diplomat. His career spanned the regimes of Louis XVI, the years of the French Revolution, Napoleon, Louis XVIII, and Louis-Philippe.

authority of the nation vested in the King acting with the advice and consent of his ministers appointed by him for their skill and capacity and in the appointments of state subject to the confidence and responsible to the freely elected and independent House of Commons. Secondly the House of Lords as the supreme court of English law acting with the advice of the English bench of judges and thirdly the supreme law enforcement authority of the nation vested in the freely elected House of Commons being the Grand Inquest of the Nation to which all authority executive administrative and judicial were finally responsible.

So constituted Parliament could never exercise a despotic and arbitrary power in that only by reason and consent can a common agreement of three independent co-ordinate institutions be established. The supremacy of Parliament thus stood as a barrier against any manifestation of arbitrary or despotic power in derogation of the fundamental rights and liberties of the English people in their lives, their property and in their vocations not only against the power of the state but against exploitation by their more powerful fellow subjects.

It was this magnificent establishment of a free legal democracy which was challenged by the modern doctrine of Parliamentary sovereignty. This doctrine was first mooted by Lord Mansfield, a Scottish Jacobite who had become Lord Chief Justice of England and an active member of the Government in the early years of the reign of George III. Under his guidance George claimed that a packed and un-representative Parliament under his control had the supreme authority above the rights and liberties of the people, a claim which resulted in the American rebellion and in the crises at home associated with Wilkes[13] and the Middlesex elections.

---

[13] **John Wilkes** (1725 – 1797) was an English radical, journalist, and politician. He was first elected Member of Parliament in 1757. In the Middlesex election dispute, he fought for the right of his voters—rather than the House of

Not only had Mansfield's influence a disrupting constitutional consequence but an equally disastrous effect on the development of English law at the most critical period of the industrial revolution in which the relationship between the rights of property and the right to vocation became completely unbalanced under the influence of the new so-called science of political economy and its doctrine of buying cheap and selling dear on a contractual basis. In these conditions the fundamental right to vocation was crushed and labour was to be treated as a commodity subject to the economic law of supply and demand.

It was the greatest single failure of the English judicial process under the leadership of Lord Mansfield that the legal relationship of master and servant was never developed to meet the new industrial conditions and no legal protection was afforded to those who depended entirely on their labour as their means of livelihood. Property, in particular industrial property, was accorded full rights without any corresponding duties regardless of established English legal principles. How far this was taken is shown by the well-known case of the American Negro slave brought from America by his master to England. The Negro appealed to Lord Mansfield for his release from his slave condition. The law of England was already clearly established for such a case. In the reign of Queen Elizabeth I a Russian serf under similar conditions was granted his freedom by the courts on the ground that the air of England is so free that no serf or slave could live in it. Yet Lord Mansfield was so obsessed with the rights of property that it was only by force of public opinion and after

---

Commons—to determine their representatives. In 1768 angry protests of his supporters were suppressed in the St George's Fields Massacre. In 1771, he was instrumental in obliging the government to concede the right of printers to publish verbatim accounts of parliamentary debates. In 1776, he introduced the first Bill for parliamentary reform in the British Parliament. During the American War of Independence, he was a supporter of the American rebels, adding further to his popularity with American Whigs.

long delays that Mansfield grudgingly ordered the release of the Negro.

"In Bagehot's day the private member (of Parliament) was free to defy the whip, genuinely responsible to his own conscience and his constituents and genuinely at liberty within wide limits to speak as he wished. It was this independence of the private member that gave the Commons its collective character and made it the most important check on the executive. Now the prime responsibility of the member is no longer to his conscience or to the elector but to his party. Without accepting the discipline of the party he cannot be elected and if he defies that discipline, he risks political death. Even forty years ago it was still possible to cross the floor and survive. But today the member who loses the whip may win the next election but after that the party will destroy him. Party loyalty has become the prime political virtue required of a Member of Parliament and the test of that loyalty is his willingness to support the official leadership when he knows it to be wrong."

Parliament now provides no check on misgovernment. The professional party politician by his control on the House of Commons has liberated himself from all constitutional restraint. This lawless irresponsible sovereignty is symbolised by the modern party Cabinet system which has no legal or constitutional standing but which by constitutional convention has replaced Parliament as the supreme national authority. Sir Ivor Jennings[14] in his standard work *"Cabinet Government"* confirms that:

"The Cabinet is the core of the British Constitutional system. It is the supreme directing power."

---

[14] **Sir William Ivor Jennings**, (1903 – 1965) was a British lawyer and academic. He was a prominent educator who served as the Vice Chancellor of University of Cambridge (1961–63) and University of Ceylon (1942–55).

Having no constitutional standing, the party Cabinet operates entirely by practices. As Sir Ivor put it:

"The whole system of Cabinet Government is founded not on laws but on practices."

How these operate Sir Ivor explained in his introduction where he pointed out that:

"The most important parts of the Cabinet system function in secret. Information is rarely made available until the persons concerned in particular events are dead. The constitutional lawyer is apt therefore to be a generation behind the times."

In fact it is impossible to know what the practices at any time are for Sir Ivor concludes his introduction by declaring that:

"The British Constitution is changing so rapidly it is difficult to keep pace with it."

This was the position as recently as 1936 when this introduction was written.

The doctrine of Parliamentary sovereignty is in fact a constitutional phantom without substance or reality but which in the words of Dicey "fosters the despotic authority of a democratic state" and "provides the argument in favour not of individual freedom but of the absolution of the state" an absolution which Dicey likened to the autocracy of the Russian Czar and which he suggested had the legal power to enact the murder of blue-eyed babies at birth.

This democracy is as illusory as the sovereignty of Parliament on which it rests. As R.T. McKenzie points out in his standard text book *"British Political Parties"*:

"Lip service is still paid to the classical conception of democracy even by many who are aware of the extent to which it has proved

unworkable. The study of the psychology of the political processes has revealed the importance of the extra-rational and irrational elements in social behaviour. The parallel development of the arts of political propaganda has enabled political leaders to exploit the irrational elements in human behaviour and to manufacture what is often a purely synthetic 'general will' so much so that some people are prepared to argue . . . that the will of the people is the product and not the motive power of the political process."

Is this not precisely the basis of the modern totalitarian party despotisms and one of the most terrible forms of autocracy known to mankind because it can claim a democratic support? The doctrine of Parliamentary sovereignty has provided the complete legal basis for precisely such an autocracy. We may now understand what Dicey meant when he wrote that:

"Parliamentary sovereignty is an instrument well adapted for the establishment of democratic despotism."

The fact that the British party system allows for a choice of political party leadership has very little significance. As Professor C. W. Keeton makes clear in *"Elementary Principles of Jurisprudence"*:

"One of the chief differences between the modern totalitarian state and Great Britain is that the latter country provides for change in the governing party, if the electorate so decide whilst the system of the totalitarian state does not. In both cases the individual is left face to face with the sovereign authority with the balance heavily against him."

But whereas the single party totalitarian system provides at least the semblance of national unity and cohesion and follows usually a stable and well-defined policy, the multi-party system rests upon national dissension as the basis of its law and government. By making national policy dependent on the rivalry of professional politicians in the exercise of the supreme power of the state national policy rests on nothing firmer than political expediency to achieve maximum electoral support regardless of long term national considerations. This rivalry of politicians for supreme power actuates passion and partisan emotion, fed by ignorance and prejudice in which basic human rights and national welfare are subject to uninhibited political ambition modified only by political expediency and gilded over with specious idealism in which injustice is exploited for purely political ends. Such a system of competition for power by the professional politicians of the different parties and within the party organization sets up a constant turmoil and turbulence in national affairs and makes impossible that stability and sense of common purpose upon which alone national and civilised progress can be attained. It is this chronic lack of stability and constant uncertainty by which national cohesion and social unity has for a century been progressively eroded.

The process begun by Lord Mansfield was taken up by the Benthamite[15] Utilitarian movement which in England and Scotland was the offshoot of French intellectual activity generated by French revolutionary ideology and which presented itself as a movement of progress and reform when it came to power after the first Parliamentary Reform Act of 1832. The Benthamite reforms were directed not to the restoration of English Common Law principles which Mansfield's influence had confused and undermined but were

---

[15] **Jeremy Bentham** (1748 - 1832) English utilitarian philosopher and social reformer. His campaign for social and political reforms in all areas, most notably the criminal law, had its theoretical basis in his utilitarianism, expounded in his *Introduction to the Principles of Morals and Legislation*, a work written in 1780 but not published until 1789. In it he formulated the principle of utility, which approves of an action in so far as an action has an overall tendency to promote the greatest amount of happiness. Happiness is identified with pleasure and the absence of pain.

directed to develop Lord Mansfield's concepts to their final and extreme conclusion.

At the time of the first Reform Act of 1832. John Austin[16], a dedicated follower of Bentham propounded his theory of law and sovereignty which was to dominate English legal and constitutional development for the next century, and provide the legal basis of political democracy drawn from French Revolutionary ideology.

The basic theme of the Austinian theory of law and sovereignty was the total rejection of all constitutional law by which the supreme authority could in any way be bound. Austinian theory thus points to an unlimited despotism as the basis of all legal authority excluding justice and equity as the purpose of law and denying any legal protection of the rights and liberties of the people in their lives, their property and vocations against the authority of the state. The sole safeguard against such a monstrous despotism was to be the policy of political democracy based upon party organization.

The rise of the modern totalitarian party dictatorships by the political democratic processes has revealed the full horrors to which Austinian theory of law and sovereignty can lead so that today we hear very little of Austinian jurisprudence. But Austinian doctrine remains the basis of our modern political system in which political democracy is identified with professional party politicians. Though Austin himself rejected the application of his theory of sovereignty to the English Parliament, it was nevertheless Austinian sovereignty which in 1885 A.V. Dicey in his lectures as professor of English Law at the University of Oxford applied to Parliament without any authority whatsoever. These lectures, now generally referred to as Dicey's "*Law of the Constitution*" are the recognized standard constitutional authority for our modern political system.

---

[16] **John Austin** (1790 – 1859) was a noted British jurist and published extensively concerning the philosophy of law and jurisprudence.

The immediate consequence of Dicey's application of Austinian sovereignty to Parliament is the total nullification of all constitutional law. In place of constitutional law, Dicey has given us the conventions of the constitution. The consequence is that what is constitutional in law can by constitutional convention be regarded as unconstitutional in practice and practices, however flagrantly illegal have to be accepted as constitutional. The constitution of Parliament itself is now not a matter of law but of constitutional convention for as Dicey has put it in the "*Law of the Constitution*":

"The conventions of the constitution now consist of customs which are at the present day maintained for the sake of ensuring the supremacy of the House of Commons and ultimately through the elective House of Commons of the nation."

In other words by constitutional convention the sovereignty of Parliament means the sovereignty of the House of Commons. But by the same conventional process, the House of Commons itself is now transformed. The first condition of a Parliamentary House of Commons is that it is freely elected and that its membership' when elected is free and independent from all influences of fear or favour. This was first confirmed in the Revolution of 1399 when Richard II was deposed for among other accusations of interfering in the freedom of elections and attempting to control the House of Commons. The same issues were present in the Revolution of 1688 when James II was forced to abdicate. This was finally and conclusively confirmed in the great Parliamentary enactment known as the Bill of Rights which still stands upon our statute book. But under the doctrine of Parliamentary sovereignty this constitutional enactment has lost its validity and the House of Commons has ceased to qualify as a Parliamentary House of Commons based upon the freedom of elections and the independence of its members. The elections to the House of Commons are now controlled by the professional party politicians who have brought its membership under their iron control. What this means was shown by R.H.S. Crossman in his 1963 introduction to Walter Bagehot's "*The English Constitution*" which first appeared in 1867. Crossman wrote:

"A political system resting on professional party politicians is clearly fatal to all liberty and national well-being. It represents a total destruction of our historic Parliamentary constitution behind whose forms, institutions and ceremonies it has disguised itself whilst at the same time rendering them meaningless. The full meaning of Parliamentary supremacy is now lost to us by the constitutional corruptions which the professional politician has fomented by their appeals to an alien and fraudulent political democratic ideology. By clearly identifying and correcting these corruptions we can recover the enduring quality of strength and freedom of our Parliamentary constitution for which generations of Englishmen have for centuries been ready to sacrifice their lives and their possessions."

THE RESTORATION OF THE ENGLISH CONSTITUTION

The greatness of English achievement in the past has been based on the readiness of her people to be guided by empirical considerations in which past experience was taken as the guide to the solution of current problems. It was the constant reliance on precedent that gave English law and government its immense strength and stability and by which England preserved the realities of civil and political freedom. The consequence is that there are no people in the civilized world today which has a greater fund of past experiences to draw upon than the English. In English law and government we have a thousand years of recorded achievement to guide us back to the practical re-establishment of the most magnificent basis of national authority in the history of mankind.

For over a century now we have allowed ideological considerations to determine our system of law and government. Walter Bagehot, the leading constitutional commentator since Burke, in his 1872 introduction to "*The English Constitution*" remarked that:

"The future of this country depends on the happy working of a delicate experiment".

Though he was referring to the consequences of the Parliamentary Reform Act of 1867, it had a wider reference to what he called "the new constitution" which in his words was "framed on the principle of choosing a single sovereign authority and making it good".

This principle of sovereignty is precisely that by which the hereditary rulers of other lands imposed their despotic authority with the difference that it was to be elective. This elective sovereignty on which Bagehot based the "new constitution" is derived from French Revolutionary ideology which had spread to England and Scotland and had become the dominant influence in the reformed Parliaments after 1832. This "new constitution" thus aimed to establish English law and government upon the political democracy of French Revolutionary ideology with a single sovereign authority.

This new principle of English law and government marked the rejection of the cardinal principle of the historic English Constitution by which all authority including the supremacy of Parliament was subject to God and the law based upon the process of judicial reason and consent. This fundamental break with our constitutional past was however obscured by the retention of its forms, institutions and ceremonies. These symbols of our historic constitution were described by Bagehot as the "*dignified parts*" and retained only to "excite and preserve the reverence of the population" and thus to disguise what Bagehot called "*the efficient parts*" by which the "new constitution" actually "works and rules".

Bagehot was quite open in this deception by which the English people were deprived of their great constitutional heritage. He declared that the English monarchy was to do nothing more than to:

"*...act as disguise. It enables our real rulers to change without heedless people knowing it. The masses of Englishmen are not fit for an elective government; if they knew how near they were to it, they would be surprised and almost tremble.*"

In another passage he again reverts to the secret changes that the "new constitution" had carried through when he declared that:

"*The appendages of the monarchy have been converted into the essence of a republic, only here, because of a more numerous heterogeneous political population, it is needful to keep the ancient show while we secretly interpolate the new reality."*

It was the enlargement by the Reform Act of 1867 of the number of those who could elect the sovereign authority which caused Bagehot considerable unease. As a follower of Hobbes, Bagehot entirely endorsed the principle of a single sovereign authority but he had misgivings for such a sovereign authority being chosen by a mass electorate through disciplined political parties which were then being established. As he pointed out:

"The only mode by which a cohesive majority and lasting administration can be upheld in a Parliamentary Government is party organization but that organization itself tends to aggravate party violence and party animosity. It is in substance subjecting the whole nation to the rule of a section of the nation, selected because of its speciality. Parliamentary Government is, in its essence a sectarian government and is possible only when sects are cohesive."

How far such cohesion could be maintained with the enlarged electorate constituted the "delicate experiment" to which Bagehot referred. As he pointed out:

"If the first work of the poor voter is to try and create a poor man's Paradise,... the great political trial now beginning will simply fail."

The principle of a single elective sovereign authority was confirmed in 1885 when Professor A.V. Dicey formulated the doctrine of Parliamentary Sovereignty which on his sole authority has been received as the fundamental principle of Parliamentary Democracy in Britain. The implications of this doctrine, Dicey revealed in 1905 when he declared that:

"Parliamentary Sovereignty is an instrument well adapted for the establishment of democratic despotism."

With the rise in more recent times of the modern totalitarian party dictatorships we know what democratic despotism can lead to and which is today giving ever growing concern as to the direction of modern Parliamentary democracy in Britain.

To meet the unfolding threat which Parliamentary Sovereignty portends, there is proposed to us a new Bill of Rights, a written constitution and electoral reform. But as long as Parliamentary sovereignty is accepted as the active factor in our political system, all such proposals are meaningless. How in the face of Parliamentary sovereignty can a new Bill of Rights have any more effective force than the great Bill of Rights now upon the statute book? How can a written constitution be more effective than our historic constitution which is still the supreme law of the land? How can electoral reform to improve the representation of minority opinion strengthen the authority of Parliament when the end and purpose of the modern party system is to eliminate and suppress the free representative quality of the House of Commons which the great Bill of Rights now on the statute book was intended to guarantee?

The fundamental fact remains that the doctrine of Parliamentary Sovereignty abrogates all constitutional law including that which governs the constitution of Parliament itself. The doctrine of Parliamentary sovereignty is in fact directed to destroy the legal supremacy of Parliament, the corner stone of our historic constitution. The legal supremacy of Parliament is based upon the common agreement in a written form of the three independent co-ordinate institutions of the King, the House of Lords and the House of Commons. We have allowed the political democracy of French Revolutionary ideology to blind us to the great stabilizing qualities of the English monarchy and its Privy Council both of which are now reduced to constitutional cyphers. With perversity we have degraded the House of Lords by swelling to inordinate proportions its hereditary membership with the sale of honours and the grant of titles for political and partisan purposes[17]. We have allowed the same ideology to enhance the party packed House of Commons as the residual embodiment of the mythical popular will which French Revolutionary ideology postulates as the basis of all authority, so much so that the doctrine of Parliamentary sovereignty has come to mean in practice the sovereignty of the House of Commons alone.

This is not the first time in English history that a claim to omnipotence has been put forward by the House of Commons. On January 4th, 1649 the packed rump of the House of Commons resolved:

"The Commons of England in Parliament assembled to declare that the people are under God, the original of all power. And also declare that the Commons of England in Parliament assembled being chosen by and representing the people, have the supreme power of the nation. And also declare "that whatever is enacted or declared for law by the Commons in Parliament assembled hath the force of law and all the people of this nation are concluded hereby although the consent of King or House of Peers be not had thereunto."

This resulted in the setting up of a republican government under the title of "The Keepers of the Liberty of England by Authority of Parliament" in which Parliament meant the House of Commons alone.

What was the consequence of this assumption of supreme power by the House of Commons? Oliver Cromwell who played a leading part in the setting up of the new political system less than three years later said:

"As for the Members of Parliament, their pride and ambition and self seeking, ingrossing all places of honour and profit to themselves and

---

[17] Today, the Hereditary Lords are all but purged from the House of Lords, and their places filled by political appointees and lackeys of the political establishment.

their friends and their daily breaking forth into new and violent parties and factions, their delay of business and designs to perpetuate themselves and to continue the power in their own hands, their meddling in private matters between man and man, contrary to the institution of Parliament and their injustice and partiality in these matters and the scandalous lives of some of the chief of them, these things do give too much ground for the people to open their mouths against them and to dislike them. Nor can they be kept within the bounds of justice, law and reason, they themselves being the supreme power of the nation liable to no account to any nor to be controlled or regulated by any other power there being none supreme or co-ordinate with them. So that unless there be some authority and power so full and so high as to restrain and keep things in better order and that there be a check on these exorbitances, it will be impossible to prevent the ruin of the nation."

This was Oliver Cromwell's justification for the military dictatorship which he set up with the government by major generals.

Today the evils of an omnipotent party packed House of Commons are even greater than those of the Cromwellian period. With a party system in which supreme authority is determined by the conflict of opposing ideologies, the all powerful House of Commons has resulted in a chronic instability in our national affairs arising from the turbulent rivalry of political factions, each alternately exercising supreme power as the result of the capricious support of a mass uninformed and bemused electorate. The result is that within a century, the most powerful industrial mercantile and financial nation in history, governed on principles of civil and political liberty by which progressive thought throughout the civilised world was guided and inspired is reduced to an impoverished impotence, with its people over taxed and over regulated.

What is even worse, Parliamentary democracy based upon the doctrine of Parliamentary sovereignty has led to a creeping lawlessness in all aspects of national authority. A.V. Dicey, the sole authority for the doctrine of Parliamentary sovereignty recognized this debilitating evil as long ago as 1914 when he wrote:

"The ancient veneration of the Rule of Law in England suffered during the last thirty years a marked decline. The truth of this assertion is proved by actual legislation, by the existence among some classes of a certain distrust both of the law and of the judges and a marked tendency towards the use of lawless methods for the attainment of social and political ends."

Dicey then further pointed out that:

"The justification of lawlessness is also in England at any rate suggested if not caused by the misdevelopment of party government. The rule of party cannot be permanently identified with the authority of the nation or with the dictates of patriotism. This fact has become so patent that eminent thinkers are to be found who certainly use language which implies that the authority or sovereignty of the nation, or even the conception of a national will, is a sort of political or metaphysical fiction which wise men do well to discard."

If Dicey is the accepted authority for the doctrine of Parliamentary sovereignty, then his authority is equally binding as to the lawless consequences to which it has led. His words point to one thing and one thing only namely that the age of ideological conflict is passed. Initiated by the era which led to the French Revolution, it has left behind it a record of violence and destructive bitterness comparable to that of the age of religious conflict by which it was preceded. Both have maimed and poisoned the foundations of western civilization. Today we can clearly recognize that the conflict of political ideologies as the basis of national authority has become meaningless in that it now merely disguises the personal ambitions of the professional party politicians and the influence of vested interests in the conduct of national affairs. Where in all other fields of human activity, ability, experience and above all character are the decisive qualities in achievement and progress, only in the public exercise of national authority do we tolerate a system based upon unrealistic ideological conflict to determine our destiny and welfare.

We are facing today the final consequences of Bagehot's "delicate experiment". We have now no framework of national authority other than a legally undefined and discredited doctrine of Parliamentary Democracy by which legitimacy is granted to any subversive ideology, however alien by which the cohesion of the English nation is being undermined. Under the guise of the "dignified parts" of our historic constitution, the "efficient parts" by which Parliamentary Democracy works and rules is in contempt of the government and constitution of this realm as by law established.

To this there can be only one answer — namely the restoration of our great constitutional heritage based upon the free system of English law made by the consent of her people and symbolized by the legal supremacy of the High Court of Parliament. The enduring strength of this heritage through the centuries lay in its resiliency in adapting itself to the changing conditions of the nation, not by the so-called constitutional conventions based upon party political expediency but by the legislative authority of a legally constituted Parliament. So today by restoring the legal supremacy of Parliament, in which the people of England are freely represented, the frame-work of national authority can be modernized on the rocklike foundation of the Rule of Law as it has ever been understood in England.

RESTORE OUR CONSTITUTION!

Today the country is governed entirely by private organisations under no legal or public control. These organisations are the political parties.

The whole object of the constitution under which we became a great nation was to lay down exactly who was to exercise the national authority, and under what conditions. Under the party system only the parties say who is to exercise authority, and there are no conditions save subservience to party. In other words the whole of our national existence is now determined by private interests.

It was in the General Election of 1874 that the modern party under caucus control became a decisive influence in our parliamentary constitution. In 1906 it achieved complete power. From 1906 onwards, constitutional law meant nothing, and everything was decided in a secret, irresponsible party committee which we know as the Cabinet.

The record of Party Government has shown a steady decline in the quality of national leadership, which has now led us into the greatest crisis in our national existence.

The supreme object of the English constitution was to ensure that the government of the country was directed solely to national ends. The aim of the constitution was to the appointment of men of the highest ability and integrity; those men were responsible to a freely elected Parliament. This responsibility was a legal responsibility, in that they could be impeached and put on trial for any dereliction or malfeasance of power. Parliament was constitutionally watching the Government to see that it carried out its duties. Grievances, and anything that went wrong in the country, could be raised in Parliament, and by control of finance and threats of impeachment redress could be obtained. The key to this system was freedom of election, which means freedom to nominate and also the freedom of the Member when elected, who is then responsible solely to the people who elected him.

When, therefore, the King nominated certain individuals to high office, he could choose anybody in the whole country, and, if he chose a Member of Parliament, that M.P. would have to resign his seat. The result was that the greatest ability and wisdom was available in the service of the country, and a Minister like Lord Burghley[18] in the reign of Elizabeth I held office for 40 years. But all these Ministers had to have the confidence of the House of Commons, the membership of which they could not control, and which could put them on trial at any time.

What is more, if the King chose someone for reasons of favouritism or otherwise unsuitable, he could never become a Minister without the House of Commons approving him.

Freedom of election and the independence of Members of Parliament is therefore the key to all that is great in our constitution, and that is why so many constitutional issues were fought over the independence of the House of Commons against the influence of the Crown in appointing Ministers who could not get the approval of a free Parliament.

The position today is that the parties, by destroying the freedom of election, now control the House of Commons. By this control the only Ministers who can gain the confidence of the House of Commons are

---

[18] **William Cecil**, 1st Baron Burghley (1520 – 1598) was an English statesman. He was the chief advisor of Queen Elizabeth I for most of her reign, twice Secretary of State (1550–1553 and 1558–1572) and Lord High Treasurer from 1572.

the party leaders themselves. By their control of the House of Commons, they can never be impeached.

Impeachment is the prosecution of Ministers by the House of Commons before the House of Lords as the Supreme Court for any mistakes, neglect of duty, or betrayal of the national interest.

The Minister could not avoid impeachment by hiding under any Cabinet secrecy, or theory of collective responsibility, which the party system has introduced to-day into our constitution. By controlling the House of Commons, the parties are now able to appoint their own members as ministers, and these ministers are only responsible to their own party organisation. They are never impeached, and they can conduct the government of the country without any serious check.

PARTY RESPONSIBILITY

All major parties are responsible for destroying the freedom of Parliament, and they have made constitutional government impossible. The only way to restore constitutional government is to restore the freedom of the M.P. This means that the political monopoly established by the parties in nominating candidates must be destroyed. It means further that the whole concept of party government must be destroyed, and that constitutional government in Britain must be based on national principles. Without such a constitutional basis of government, there can be no national recovery.

If you vote for a party candidate, you are voting for unconstitutional government. In your constituency, you should choose men who will support the legal constitution and represent you as independent people in Parliament. A free Parliament is the only way to achieve a free Britain.

The most immediate interest for our country is now to elect a free Parliament. It is not possible to put up independent candidates now because the parties (since the 1918 war) have imposed a penalty of

£150[19] on what they call "frivolous"—in other words independent—candidates. For Britons to achieve their freedom, every constituency should hold a nomination conference, and, until this law has been changed, they should set up a fund to provide their independent candidates with the necessary money to pay their deposits. They should then see to it that they choose *independent* candidates for Parliament. Forty to fifty independent M.P.s could end party government by making a House of Commons majority impossible, leaving constitutional government as the only alternative.

The qualifications for an independent candidate must be:

Allegiance to the Queen;

Acceptance of the legal constitution;

Political views and principles but no set political programme;

Integrity and reputation sufficient to satisfy the electors of his sincerity in professions of loyalty;

Undertaking to oppose *every* government appointed by a party;

Undertaking to support only those Ministers appointed by the Crown of whose suitability he is satisfied—i.e. no collective appointments;

Undertaking that he himself while an M.P. will refuse any office, and

Undertaking to make himself acquainted with all grievances and to air them adequately.

In the fourth part of *The Institutes of the Laws of England Concerning the Jurisdiction of Courts* by the great Edward Coke[20], J.C., there

---

[19] Today this is £500.

[20] **Sir Edward Coke** (1552 – 1634) was an English barrister, judge and, later, opposition politician, who is considered to be the greatest jurist of the Elizabethan and Jacobean eras.

appears the following definition of: "What properties a Parliament Man should have".

PROPERTIES OF THE ELEPHANT

"It appeareth in a Parliament Roll, that the Parliament being as hath been said, called commune concilium, every Member of the House being a councillor, should have three properties of the elephant; first that he hath no gall; secondly, that he is inflexible, and cannot bow; thirdly, that he is of a most ripe and perfect memory; which properties as there it is said, ought to be in every Member of the Great Council of Parliament.

"First, to be without gall that is, without malice, rancour, heat, and envy, in elephante melancholia transit in nutrimentum corporis. Every gallish inclination (if any were) should tend to the good of the whole body and commonwealth.

"Secondly, that he be constant, inflexible, and not to be bowed, or turned from the right, either for fear, reward or favour, nor in judgement respect any person.

"Thirdly, of a ripe memory, that they remembering perils past, might prevent dangers to come, as in that Roll of Parliament appeareth. Whereunto we will add two other properties of the elephant, the one that though they be Maximae virtutis et maximi intellectus, of greatest strength and understanding, tamen gregatim semper incedunt, yet they are sociable and goe in companies; for animalia gregalia non sunt nociva, sed animalia solivaga sunt nociva. Sociable creatures that goe in flocks or herds are not hurtful, as deer, sheep, etc., but beasts that walk solely, or singularly, as bears, foxes, etc., are dangerous and hurtful.

"The other that the elephant is philanthropos, homini erranti viam osteredit, and these properties ought every Parliament Man to have."

CONSTITUTIONAL RIGHTS DESTROYED

In Great Britain today there is no recognised Constitutional law as the result of the reception of Austinian jurisprudence. As Sir Ivor Jennings, in his standard text book *The Law and the Constitution*, points out:

"Strictly speaking there is no constitutional law at all in Great Britain. There is only the arbitrary power of Parliament."

In consequence, Englishmen have now no Constitutional rights. As Lord Wright said in an historic judgment in the House of Lords (Liversedge v. Anderson):

"In the Constitution of England there are no guaranteed or absolute rights. The safeguard of British liberty is the good sense of the people and the system of representative and responsible Government which has been evolved."

This "representative and responsible Government" is the Party Cabinet, which has no legal foundations and is completely controlled by the private political party system. In Britain today, the will of the party with a majority has the force of absolute law.

As they are private organisations under no public control we know nothing about these party machines, which for fifty[21] years now have replaced our legal Constitution. They claim, however, that their authority is democratic because they have been elected.

The position is that the party system has no legal standing for such a claim. The parties have achieved this power by bringing the

---

[21] The author was writing in 1956.

membership of the House of Commons under disciplined control by methods which are in direct contravention of the greatest of all our Constitutional enactments the Bill of Rights, whereby the freedom of election is protected. As, under modern jurisprudence, there is no Constitutional law, the Bill of Rights, and with it the freedom of electors, has lost all validity. It is by virtue of our "representative system of Government" that we have lost our Constitutional rights.

ESSENCE OF FREEDOM

The essence of freedom of election lies in the freedom of nomination of candidates and freedom of the elected representative from all influences of fear or favour. Today we have no freedom of nomination. This is entirely a party system monopoly. Freedom of election under such conditions can be judged by the declaration of Boss Tweed[22], the founder of Tammany Hall:

"I believe in the freedom of election as a constitutional right. I do not care who does the electing, just so as I do the nominating."

Our position in Britain today has been described by the late L.S. Amery[23] in his *Thoughts on the Constitution*:

"At a General Election the voter is in no position to choose either the kind of representative . . . he would like if he had a choice. . . . The candidates before him, the only candidates worth taking seriously, are

---

[22] **William Magear Tweed** (1823 – 1878) widely known as "Boss" Tweed – was an American politician most notable for being the "boss" of Tammany Hall, the Democratic Party political machine that played a major role in the politics of 19th century New York City and State.

[23] **Leopold Charles Maurice Stennett Amery** (1873 – 1955), was a British Conservative Party politician and journalist, noted for his interest in military preparedness, India, and the British Empire. He is perhaps best remembered today for his famous attack, quoting Cromwell, in Parliament on Neville Chamberlain in 1940 "You have sat too long here for any good you have been doing. Depart, I say, and let us have done with you. In the name of God, go!"

either supporters of the team in office or of its rivals for office. It is within these narrow limits that his actual power is exercised."

Once elected, the party members fall under the control of the party whip, and they are subject to control by party central offices which may question them and coerce them regarding their votes, speeches and activities in Parliament. No King of England has ever so usurped the privileges of Parliament in such flagrant contempt of the Bill of Rights.

BURKE'S WARNING

The party system has destroyed our Parliament. As Burke has put it in his *Present Discontents*:

"For my part I shall be compelled to conclude the principle of Parliament to be totally corrupted and therefore its ends entirely defeated when I see two symptoms: first, a rule of indiscriminate support to all Ministers; because this destroys the very end of Parliament as a control, and is a general previous sanction to misgovernment; and secondly, the setting up of any claims adverse to the right of free election, for this tends to subvert the legal authority by which the House of Commons sits."

It is still open to us to restore the freedom of Parliament, and with it our Constitutional system, by the active restoration of the freedom of election. Above all we need to reject our modern jurisprudence, and re-affirm the fundamental principles of our Constitution.

About Ben Greene

By Tregunta Cathcart and Rob Black

Born in Santos, Brazil on the 28th December 1901, Ben was the eldest of the six siblings of Edward Greene, a coffee merchant and Eva Stutzer, a German national. Moving to England in 1909, he attended Berkhamsted School in Hertfordshire, where his uncle Charles was headmaster and his cousins Graham and Hugh attended as pupils along with A.K. Chesterton.

Awkward in demeanour and only average at his studies, this gentle boy, generous and kindly by temperament, and with a genuine concern for those less fortunate than himself, had expressed from an early age his ambition to become an engineer at a railway workshop or failing that, a Royal Engineer, where he imagined he would get 'good pay and free food!'

He went up to Wadham College, Oxford in 1920, ostensibly to read history but soon found himself disillusioned with university life in general and indifferent to the Oxford milieu, becoming, due to his concerns with the problems of the world at large, both a socialist and a Quaker with a passion for pacifism.

Though in touch with the Labour Party at this time, he had an aversion to doctrinaire socialism and found his natural home in the Independent Labour Party, with its roots going back to the Chartist and non-conformist movements, along with its marked influence from the Christian socialism of men like Ruskin and Charles Kingsley.

Greene was soon to be doubly conflicted, first by his German born mother's dislike of her native country's arrogant militarism and also by the loss of so many of his masters and school fellows during the Great War. Outraged by what he perceived has the ingratitude shown to returning service-men 'in a land fit for heroes', he seized the opportunity, while still at Oxford, to visit Germany and undertook relief work for the Quakers, which gave him first-hand experience of how unfair the Treaty of Versailles actually was to the German people, leading him to the conclusion that it could only lead to a second continental conflagration - as was proved the case in 1939.

During vacations from Oxford, Ben undertook relief work in Warsaw, Krakow, Danzig and along the Polish Corridor, coordinating the charitable work of both the Quakers and the Save the Children Charity.

Eventually dropping out of Oxford in 1923, without completing his degree, he spent a year in Russia with the American Relief Commission administered by the Society of Friends, distributing aid to famine stricken regions.

Recognizing the total failure of organized Christianity to face up to the moral issues which the war produced and informed by his recent activities in Europe and Russia, he joined the Labour Party upon his return to England, giving public speeches the length and breadth of the country, before standing on the Party ticket in Basingstoke and Gravesend and becoming the prospective parliamentary candidate for South West Hull. During this period he was instrumental in forming the Constituency Party Association in the Labour Party, advocating for direct representation from the constituency parties onto the Labour Executive Committee. However, by pursuing such a policy he came into heated conflict with the Labour Leadership and was threatened with expulsion on more than one occasion.

In 1925 he married Leslie Campbell[24] and entered his father's own Kepston's Company which specialized in wooden pulleys and other products involving the turning of wood. This, his father hoped, would provide a settled life for his errant son, but Ben had little interest in or aptitude for business and found himself in regular need of financial assistance throughout this and future entrepreneurial periods of his career.

By the time of the Saar Plebiscite in 1935, Ben, who had been appointed a JP in 1936 and was to serve a total of six years on Berkhamsted District Council and two years on the Hertfordshire County Council, was chosen as the Chief Deputy Returning Officer by the League of Nations, and soon after the vote was sent out to the Saar, on behalf once again, of the Society of Friends to investigate reported cases relating to the ill-treatment of Jews in the area.

After the November pogroms of 1938, he was heavily involved in the organisation of relief for the Jewish population resident in Germany and was arrested by the Gestapo, only to be released through the direct intervention of a sympathetic German official.

Soon after his return to Britain, Greene found himself in dispute with the Labour Party Executive once more, this time over his proposal to take a delegation of Trade Unionists to Germany following an invitation from the Mayor of Saarbrucken. The visit, to review the conditions of the German workers, was prohibited and he reluctantly acquiesced to the Executive Committee's decision.

At the time of the Munich crisis, Greene found himself so diametrically opposed to the foreign policy of the Labour Party that he felt compelled to resign, consequently relinquishing his candidature of South West Hull. Willing to work with anyone who

---

[24] This marriage produced two daughters, Ann and Margaret 'Leslie' Greene. Leslie Greene was heavily involved with *Candour* and the League of Empire Loyalists in the 1950's and 1960's.

sought to maintain peace in Europe, Ben soon found himself in what would later be characterized as 'dubious company', people such as the Marquis of Tavistock[25], a leading world expert on parrots and budgerigars and John Beckett[26], both of whom were active in the British People's Party (BPP). As a consequence he was bitterly attacked by the Labour leadership for being 'pro-Nazi', despite the obvious fact that he was a Quaker and an active pacifist. For Ben, the simplistic knee-jerk response to revert to militarism in order to defeat Germany seemed a blunt instrument, and he made it clear there were a whole range of aspects to the Nazi regime which were repugnant to both his religious and social convictions.

Indeed, he caused consternation within the BPP over his stance on anti-Semitism, stemming from the Party's manifesto which included references to the abolition of the financial system based on usury, constraints on financial speculators, protection for labour in industrial disputes, freeing parliament from vested interest groups in the economic or geopolitical sphere and safeguarding British people from alien influences and infiltration of its organs and instruments of state.

By January 1939, Greene who later maintained he had been a minor figure within the BPP, despite providing an office for the BPP Secretary John Beckett at his Kepston's facility in Berkhamstead, had formed the *Peace & Progressive Information Service*, to counter what he perceived as the Communist subversion within the Labour Party. The service managed to produce sixteen regular bulletins on international affairs to subscribers before the operation was wound up.

---

[25] **Hastings Russell** (1888 – 1953). Later the **12th Duke of Bedford**. According to his son "He loved birds, animals, peace, monetary reform, the park and religion."

[26] **John Beckett** (1894 – 1964) was a leading figure in British politics between the world wars, both in the Labour Party and the Fascist movements.

As an opponent both of communism and fascism, he felt no foreign ideological system should be implemented in Britain and had originally joined the BPP, on the principle that it stood on a platform of parliamentary reform. However, in the face of open hostilities on the Polish German border, he still advocated for a negotiated peace, but realizing that there was no real possibility of affecting a settlement, he resigned from the BPP and all other political activities, returning to the management of his business.

By now Kepston's was the solitary wood-split pulley factory in Britain and was listed as conducting work of national importance. Given that its European rivals were now cut off from the British market it was enjoying a form of monopoly status and would no doubt have kept Ben at least occupied, if not stimulated, had it not been for his detention under the notorious Defence Regulation 18B, which saw many Britons detained and held without trial.

This despite the fact that for over twenty years, as a Quaker, and later as a member of the Meeting of Sufferings, he had been consistent in both his social and political activities and had worked tirelessly for international peace, and at home for the improvement of social conditions along democratic lines.

The order to arrest Greene was signed on the 23rd May 1940 and he was seized on the 24th May. The 'Reasons for Order' cited Greene's membership of the BPP, the content of his speeches, his association with John Beckett, and his communication with the German government.

Further allegations were made against him by a German double agent named Harald Kurtz who entrapped Greene with another M15 agent, Friedl Gartner, as witness, and alleged that Greene had helped him to avoid further internment and clandestinely communicated with Germany, and had told him ways of leaving the country undetected. Kurtz also claimed that Greene had said that there were 'men in this country ready to take over the government after a German victory, men trained in and filled with the proper spirit of National Socialism- a British National Socialism'.

Greene denied these allegations and claimed that he had reported Kurtz's suspicious behaviour to the police. The police denied this element of Greene's defence, keeping him in horrendous conditions, while he began to work on his book on the British Constitution. After one visit, his daughters found conditions so foul, they were reduced to tears. Margaret vowed never to go again. Despite the conditions, he was popular with both prison staff and inmates.

His initial appeal for release, made at a time when he was still unaware of the reasons for his incarceration, but became clearer once his written appeal was submitted and subsequently failed, was a major set-back. However, his brother Edward secured a solicitor, Oswald Hickson, who was experienced in representing other internees and therefore familiar with the legal intricacies involved in such matters. Once Hickson got to work on the case, it became abundantly clear that Harald Kurtz was in fact a M15 agent provocateur, discrediting his testimony in the process and partly exonerating Ben, so that the detention order was revoked on the 9th January 1942, with the proviso that he would avoid contact with undesirable characters like 12th Duke of Bedford and John Beckett, who recalled Greene as "having a sort of constant melancholy lying under his surface panache. His size making him something of an outsider". He was also obliged not to hinder the war effort in any way.

Embittered by the experience, Greene tried to sue for damages and false imprisonment but the action was withdrawn on the advice of his counsel, though still nearly bankrupting him with costs of £1,243.

Unsurprisingly, Greene was now suffering from a persecution complex which marked his remaining days. Leaving Kepston's to be managed by others, he moved his family to Braefoot in Kinross-shire, where, because he was a man of some energy and perseverance, he set up and manufactured furnaces to take advantage of a pioneering development in hydrogen cooled heating systems. Soon his company was filling supply orders from giant American companies from the very heart of rural Scotland, but his entrepreneurial ineptitude still meant the company teetered on the brink of bankruptcy, only narrowly surviving a crisis in 1954 because of the direct intervention of his brothers, Felix and Edward.

By now he had re-entered the political sphere, associating himself with the English National Association dedicated to restoring the liberties outlined in the Magna Carta.

Following his retirement, he continued to brood over the injustices of his internment, but was fortunate enough to have inherited a house in Cambridge-shire which relieved him of pressing financial distress. In his later years he continued to work on his book on the British Constitution, but when he passed away on the 17th March 1978, the manuscript was still incomplete.

Sources

The information on Ben Greene in the final chapter of this book has mainly come from "*Shades of Greene - One Generation of an English Family*" by Jeremy Lewis, and published by Jeremy Cape in 2010. Also consulted was "*The Rebel Who Lost His Cause*" by Francis Beckett, published by London House in 1999.

Other details have come from the journal *The Word*, May 1941 and February 1942.

About The A.K. Chesterton Trust

The A.K. Chesterton Trust was formed by Colin Todd and the late Miss. Rosine de Bounevialle in January 1996 to succeed and continue the work of the now defunct Candour Publishing Co.

The objects of the Trust are stated as follows:

"To promote and expound the principles of A.K. Chesterton which are defined as being to demonstrate the power of, and to combat the power of International Finance, and to promote the National Sovereignty of the British World."

Our aims include:

- *Maintaining and expanding the range of material relevant to A.K. Chesterton and his associates throughout his life.*

- *To preserve and keep in-print important works on British Nationalism in order to educate the current generation of our people.*

- *The maintenance and recovery of the sovereign independence of the British Peoples throughout the world.*

- *The strengthening of the spiritual and material bonds between the British Peoples throughout the world.*

- *The resurgence at home and abroad of the British spirit.*

We will raise funds by way of merchandising and donations.

We ask that our friends make provision for *The A.K. Chesterton Trust* in their will.

The A.K. Chesterton Trust has a **<u>duty</u>** to keep *Candour* in the ring and punching.

CANDOUR: To defend national sovereignty against the menace of international finance.

CANDOUR: To serve as a link between Britons all over the world in protest against the surrender of their world heritage.